TRACK

Annemarie Austin was born in Devon and grew up on the Somerset Levels and in Weston-super-Mare, where has lived for most of her life. She won the Cheltenham Literature Festival Poetry Competition in 1980, and her first collection, *The Weather Coming* (1987), was a Poetry Book Society Recommendation. *Very: New & Selected Poems* (Bloodaxe Books, 2008) includes work from all her previous books, including *On the Border* (1993), *The Flaying of Marsyas* (1995), *Door Upon Door* (1999) and *Back from the Moon* (2003), as well as a new collection, *Very* (2008). This was followed by her latest collection, *Track* (2014).

ANNEMARIE AUSTIN

Track

BLOODAXE BOOKS

ISBN: 978 1 85224 992 2

First published 2014 by
Bloodaxe Books Ltd,
Highgreen,
Tarset,
Northumberland NE48 1RP.

www.bloodaxebooks.com
For further information about Bloodaxe titles
please visit our website or write to
the above address for a catalogue.

Supported by
**ARTS COUNCIL
ENGLAND**

Cover design: Neil Astley & Pamela Robertson-Pearce.

Printed in Great Britain by Bell & Bain Limited, Glasgow, Scotland, on
acid-free paper sourced from mills with FSC chain of custody certification.

ACKNOWLEDGEMENTS

Acknowledgements are due to the following publications where some of these poems first appeared: *Ambit, The Dark Horse, Magma, Modern Poetry in Translation, The Rialto* and *How I Land: Oxford Poets and Exiled Writers* (Heaventree Press, 2009).

'Cremated Girl' was a prizewinner in the 2012 Cardiff International Poetry Competition.

CONTENTS

11 Thrones, Principalities and Powers
12 The News
14 Else Where
15 Where We Lay Our Scene
16 Landscape with Figure
17 Those Transparent
18 New Timetable
19 Stock-still Horses
20 Night Piece with Variation
22 Still Motion Studies
24 The Sick Transit of Gloria Mundy
26 Suspense
27 Familiar
28 Third Party
29 Dunnage
30 It's Not There
31 Woman in Camera
32 Living Statue
33 Just Grass
35 Outer Space
36 Kites and Planes
37 Misremembrance
38 Swallow
39 Borders
40 Glose
42 Aggression Diary
44 T.I.A.
46 The Right Side of the Cemetery
47 Going Back In
48 The Flower at Night
49 Cremated Girl
50 Slow Vocation
52 Paper Washing
54 Painting the Blind Man
55 Once in a Blue Moon
56 Here Before
59 The Last Resort

60 Figure and Variation
62 Anon in Three Postcards
64 Man Entering Boiler House
66 On the Way
68 Fox Spirit
69 The Plain Gap
70 To Mr Jones (Boiler House Keeper)
71 That Bone
72 Still Life
73 Come the Thaw
74 Dysphasias
78 Boiler House Watching

The ancients believed that the moist track left by the snail as it crept was the snail's own essence, depleting its body little by little; the farther the snail toiled, the smaller it became, until it finally rubbed itself out.

CYNTHIA OZICK

Climb Mount Fuji,
O snail,
but slowly, slowly.

ISSA

Thrones, Principalities and Powers

You have to rise high enough
to hear the dogs in the pound.
On the footbridge beside
the railway above the river
they sound upwards at you
as if from a shaft, though
air and water stretch below.

I saw him blow a bird
of glass and air. Blob first
then bubble. Next he sat
on a throne and rolled his
budding rod across its arms
to cool the incipient bird
whose tail and beak he'd
tweak into being in a moment.

But not wings. To fly out
of the pound up to the bridge.
His bird was a fat little
robin at rest, a hot-air
balloon at best. So one
of those notes from below
must spring the trap of
such glass skin and
set its splinters flying.

The News

*When the ship approached the Pelodes Lake, Thamos turned
towards land and shouted out that Great Pan had died.
No sooner had he called out the news than he was immediately
answered by hundreds of forlorn cries, from many creatures
yelling together.*

PLUTARCH

He came to this place, and was set free
in honour of Aesculapius (it says
on the stone).
         And then, and then?

The woods are thick all around, but
you come soon to the edge of Pelodes
Lake, where the creatures shall mourn
the death of Great Pan. But not yet.

Let him go from the threshold where he was
set free, and sink into those woods, wade
leaves to the leaves' end and the lake's
beginning; let him note the brown terrapin
on the half-sunk branch, see the green
frog wait akimbo in that same dark pool
with its mouth just at the surface as
he passes; let him feel freedom like
a new stone on his tongue that keeps
the mouth moist through a long journey.

*

A mallard, wading the shallow
rapids, turns over rubbish and
turns over rubbish with its bill
like a polished shoehorn. For Pan
is dead.

Without him, feral dogs are
quartering the spread-out tip. A cow
mouths a plastic bottle in the waste
of cement where a meadow once was.

On his Cretan tomb it said (they say)
'Here lies the woodpecker who was
also Zeus.'

The donkey that grazes in
her wooden saddle, sleeps in her
wooden saddle, mourns Great Pan.

The freed slave who emerged from
the embracing woods, has spat out
his journey stone onto the stony road.

Else Where

Else where would we go?
I believe in nuance, but
here or not here cannot be
finessed. The dichotomy's
as bald as a washed egg.

For seven days of mourning
a dim light showed white
linen in the *shtetl* window,
and neighbours brought them
only a hardboiled egg to eat;

'round, with no beginning and
no end,' wrote Joseph Roth of
this objectified pain. That
was there then. The mourners
in stockinged feet have gone.

Creep away. That direction's
not finite but an always
other. She was last seen on
all fours on her path into
the mist, as in a scene

from *The Yellow Wallpaper*'s
hallucinations. In dreams
the other routes begin, where
the beach is soft with foot-
prints going every which way.

What to choose in the yellow
scrambling? Dichotomy's
gone by the board that was
an interim trestle table
for all of us on the journey.

Where We Lay Our Scene

I heard some kids on the train
deplore the boredom of the scene outside
and wish for video screens beside the track
supplying animation and proper colours.

In which there's a sort of truth, for
unless you choose to look at one fixed thing –
even if fixing is only for a moment –
it slides past almost formless in a dream

of green things interlaced with sunlight and
undercut by shade and rearings up at
the corner of the eye or land thrown down
behind a hedge to thwart any spy

such as I am in the ferry going upstream.
Now I have seen the shot tower close up
lifting from the embanked dock like a drum
on a stalk, after years in which it floated

along the built horizon as my train approached
that Bristol station and I never could fix
on its location. Filling the channel with
its wake, an arrow swan comes head on.

Landscape with Figure

I can't figure the landscape's
inbreath outbreath
at this intersection of woman
with grass trees graves path

It seems an either or
and looking at the woman means
landscape's become the water
to hold and show that fish

If I turn my back on the sea
I can hear it better
If I block out the woman
I see the curl of the trees

But unless I turn her to branches
she asserts herself on the path
and blanks out in her turn
even the pompous tombs

But landscape must breathe
must stretch roll over
in the grass or as grass
done for at the day's end

It must pull the shadows
into it and into it
and wipe out intersection
eating the woman up

Those Transparent

'Avoid, eye contact' and
they will become transparent.
Though etched outlines may pass,
you can see your way clear
right through to the head of the queue
in the post office, to the very end
of the pedestrian precinct.

In discount stores the discounted
under fluorescent striplights
are ghosts at midday. Piled goods
on either side the aisles
can more or less annihilate
with their emphatic substance,
and only flawed glass walks.

To be broken in the gutter maybe.
I've seen those smashed lenses
edged with blood – though probably,
as with the fairies, not enough
to write their name in full and
put on visible thickness. Thin as
heat shimmer over fire, they lie.

But what's never altogether gone
claims its portion of the air.
That bird which dashed itself
to death on the plate-glass window
would never have tried to fly
through these, who make uneasy
the station platform, even begin
to reappear as they catch your eye.

New Timetable

That extra train the company had provided.
turned out to be a hybrid thing, a kind of
wyvern or gryphon, maybe even a hippogriff.

Certainly there were those who considered.
it worth a photograph. They strolled up
the platform, anoraks rustling, then turned
back upon it, wielding the impressive lens.

Only a goods-train engine, EWS, only
a sort of pullman car and other outmoded
rolling stock, slam doors and narrow windows.

But passengers waited for those doors
to open of themselves, in the stations they
scattered to the sudden wealth of coaches.
The power wagon's noise was all iron girders.

And the schoolboy who got on half way
through the journey, asked as he went along
the aisle, 'What does this train *mean*?'

I liked the spaciousness of the question,
as if it carried tunnels. Or as though the train
were glossed with transparent annotation
a boy might decipher if he concentrated.

But it's hard to hold what you're riding in
in your mind. Even such a wyvern disappears
inside anyone looking out of its windows.

Still I liked the question, wanted to find
that meaning, as a shape in my head which
satisfied imagination – train seen as method,
as velocity, length and confinement.

Then a tree passed by and took away my thought
with its blossom of rooks' nests. And a cloud
began to loom over the Levels, keeping pace.

Stock-still Horses

The frost is on the ground yet
and the horses are there,
stock-still in profile
over and over from the train,
standing up like stones
in the stream of sensation,
its steam on them.

Night Piece with Variation

1

She was putting on her glasses
to properly see the moon
in that west-facing window
at the top of the attic stairs;

but she knew she had no free will,
was just a bundle (though
of what she had forgotten),
so she was on the landing,
her glasses in her hand, by accident

or someone or something else's
design. Curiously she thought
of circuses, being trapped
in the round and round of the rings
and performing animals

flattened white by the full moon
into cut-out card shapes
pushed underneath the front door
to lie on the hall's dark parquet
till the sun pooled there.

But this was a night piece.
The light from the attic window
pressed on her like a stamp
on a brown-paper envelope.
She licked the cold glass

which tasted of old nothing,
smeared the sharp marked moonface
with her breath as well. Why
was she doing so? She'd have to ask
that other (or whatever).

2

There was glass and there was glass –
her spectacle lenses, the window –
and then the high moon in the west.

It was interesting to have arrived there
more by accident than design, her free
will – if she had it – in a back pocket

like the admission money for a circus –
seeing the elephants go round, each tail
held delicately by the trunk behind:

she could have cut an endless paper
frieze of them once. Now it was she
who was the paper; she felt she might

tear under the moon's bright pressure,
thin as she'd become from the long climb
up the stairs and stairs behind, going

down into the dark. The self was a bundle
of sensation, she remembered, and
breathed on the glass, licked her breath

from the glass. That sharp-edged satellite
which should have been reinstated, instead
grew a shimmering rim like the sun's.

Still Motion Studies

(after Lartigue)

> *What is in motion is neither in the space where it is,*
> *nor the space where it isn't.*
>
> ZENO OF ELEA

1 *Dédé*

The boy is a blur
and has two left arms.

Though told not to stir,
the boy is a blur.

Is this shimmer or shiver
in his world of alarms?

The boy is a blur
and has two left arms.

2 *Guitty*

Going full tilt ahead,
she must pull back.

A wave mines her tread
going full tilt ahead.

Now the rest have fled
from the tide's attack

going full tilt ahead
she must pull back.

3 *Boubotte*

There is no retreat
once the jump's begun.

For her dropping feet
there is no retreat.

From a wall's safe seat
into the blaze of the sun,

there is no retreat
once the jump's begun.

The Sick Transit of Gloria Mundy

To the boilerhouse with her!
For she is done for, for sure,
like a wisp of dried grass
in September walking through.

Mundy's child was fair of face,
a little gold half-sovereign
in the grass, for finding
and showing, and hoarding
in a small box on the shelf.

But not yet shelved
and the glory of the Mundys,
she was fifty profiles
passing the street's windows
and everyone looking out.

Hold back proliferation
for the moment. Its time
is coming – up the road
behind her striding figure.

Gloria is going so as to be read,
from left to right like a pen
which narrows her life story
down to one directed line.

When that line began to bud,
then branched and interwove
into a kind of lobster–pot
with her inside, she still
walked its tightrope gloriously

for a while. But she was sick
and went on in sickness,
knitting it, knit herself
into its fabric until
that could not be unpicked.

Pull how you will, it will only be
to drag her accumulated weight
along the roadside gutter
like a downed kite.

Suspense

Pirate the cat has found a feather
she gnaws and hugs and tosses
in the air. It's synecdoche, it will do
for one of the pigeons which torment her,
their puffed-up shadows flung onto
the backyard's underfoot concrete.

Our drunk woman neighbour is raging
again, all that she has not – but
should have – strung from her window
like a clothesline hung with rags.
The clatter of pigeons catches there.

I am watching a green caterpillar
hoist a white sail on its back.
At first glance. By the third look
I can see an old skin splitting
along its length, making flakes like
babies' fingernails, on the aquilegia.
(Remember the five-foot snakeskin
we discovered at Nicopolis next to
the Roman road, remember how we
puzzled to find it intact nose to tail,
elastic to the touch, a length
of old lace curtain in the grass.)

Baudrillard says there's suspense
in the fragment, but Pirate doesn't care
what pigeon dropped her feather.
(Somewhere in Bulgaria is the snake's
spine, or it's scattered all over as
little spiked bones.) The drunk woman
shouts they've stolen six inches of
her house. A white fingernail falls.

Familiar

Dear little damp foot
going without ball or heel
alongside my foot.
                I went
to the night garden supposing
you there, moist mouth
perambulating leaves.

You are so cold climbing
over my finger. One day
a freezing rain coated
the whole house with ice.
There was no way in.
When I beat on the door
no one came.
             You come
though not to my call
once rain has dissolved
your door...

It rained and rained.
The winter-flowering jasmine
died waterlogged in its pot.
And you were nowhere
for the season – or rather where
the bricks were worn, wearing
your own indoors.
             You stare
until one eye-stalk turns
away. You are faithless
I know. I have seen
the green-grey stony love-dart
dangling from your mantle
come the spring...

Third Party

I have been that third party:
the one facing the two
across the tennis net,
the one brought along
to screen the other two from view,
maybe at a party.

I have too often been that third,
misreading the signals,
believing our triangle equilateral
when I was the obtuse one
all the time,

my spread-out screen Japanese
with an elegant arc of gooseberry
not plum blossom.

Dunnage

Architect Adolf Loos announced
a gentleman had no business
looking out of his windows.

Timothy's decided that's all right.
He's staying in, drinking tea
from the blue pot, all sorts
of cardboard boxes stacked
between him and the light.

It's Not There

No one is watching the centre of the observatory.
You may thrash your tail there to your heart's
content.
      That air will still again before it finds
any figure at the glass.
            Behind the glare off window
after window something basilisk can shelter.

What is at the back of the gaze no one enquires.
The little limbic prances on its sharpest claw
while some kind of visor admires another view,

like the Degas girls whose lifted opera-glasses
block insolence that's blatant in their stares.

The eyes are glassy. 'I asked for bread and you
gave me a stone.'
         As with mirrors at Aachen
covered immediately they'd been shown the holy
things, then carried home...
            Could such reflections
still brood in the dark?
          All you know is they'd be
gone before you'd unfolded the wrapping to look
to find them.
         There's clatter of escape on the stairs.

Woman in Camera

The men sit outside cafés,
the street at their command.
The woman is in camera.

They don't know what she's doing
there, though they assume.
Seen through transparent walls,
she still might turn her back.

The woman looks at the wall.
The woman looks at the window.
She can see the street and men
outside cafés, if she desires.

The stanza is a room as well:
it closes on her, holds her.
I could let her get out
if I chose – but I don't today.

Come and watch her through
a judas hole between words:
she believes she's alone,
touching a chairback idly.

Approaching the peephole she grows
enormous, half out of sight.
Now she might think those thoughts
in privacy big as a ballroom.

Retreating from the door
to the window makes her
small. We can see her whole
in the whole of her setting

like a jewel (and as inscrutable).

The stanza just broke open.
The woman in camera is unmoved.

Living Statue

The heart of standing is you cannot fly.
WILLIAM EMPSON

It's an odd kind of living
to earn your living
pretending to be lifeless
outside a large museum
in a size-stiffened sheet
like John Donne in his shroud

like a lightning-conductor
in thrall to all weathers
or a tall bollard stationed
to stop nothing going on
or great exclamation mark
punctuating motion

The point is to be plinth
right to the eyelashes
to seem to have stepped
into a petrifying spring
and fossilised upwards
until a standing stone

and that's the cover story
Underneath my gaze does not
even graze the visual field
but stands knee deep
in visual grass and feels
its edges playing in the wind

Behind my eyes is space
and wild bees through the grasses
are looking for such a place
with narrow entrance and
width behind for brood
like breeding thoughts

Just Grass

*Writing of Middle Assyrian law, Gerda Lerner notes that
when veils were worn only by respectable women, 'a harlot
who presumed to appear veiled on the street was as great
a threat to social order as was the mutinous soldier or slave'.*

Taped-off
    odd-shaped
       taped-off.
          The mind goes round
            and round
at the sight.
     Is this the middle of Assyria?

The tape on stalks
      marks off
        just grass.
But just grass
     is impossible
       where there is
tape on stalks.

     Someone has presumed
to pace out the edges
      of the odd-shaped
space
   to plant stakes
      for tying tape to.
Someone has hung the tape like garlands.

Just
grass
inside
tape:
   its blades stand straight
        bend over
in every direction
     lie down on the earth

as grass outside the tape does
                              unregarded.
This is Assyria, lady.

                    There's a silk tent
of implication
                  letting its fabric down
so the hem
              can trace
                      an odd-shaped
                                space:
just grass taped-off
                    and place beyond
for anyone who comes to look at it.

'Will what's not seen
                      inside
                            get out?'
'Will whatever's been
                    held back
                    at last
                        rush in?'

Outer Space

God made everything out of nothing. But the
nothingness shows through.
PAUL VALÉRY

I was five days and nights with
outer space adjacent in the
shape of a room in Sligo off
another room in Sligo through
the thin door across a corner on
the edge of which one morning
bright was suddenly then gone.

Since the Magic Eye picture was
all spots and dapples like moving
water when it hooks the light,
and the speckled mirror just
the same, I recognised the room
next to my bed, for the puzzle-
picture's label read 'Outer Space'.

Mungo Thompson, I love your name
and how you said 'let there be'
in that gallery white where black
had been between the stars before,
and colours of outer space became
their opposites, estranging us still
more who wandered as comets do.

Kites and Planes

That morning I'd read the page from Coleridge's notebook in which he watches a 'noble' kite hover for ages 'somewhere over Mr Banks's', then turns the other way to see two kites. But those in the end are revealed as a pair of winglike leaves, the last on a fruit tree only six feet off. His long watching the floating bird had imposed its likeness on those other things in the world.

Then what made me sit up suddenly at seeing a small brown bird land with flustered noisy feet on the pavement outside the Avenue Café – to discover it was really a plane leaf twisted to a kind of cup and skittering past? Only afterwards did I start to notice how many plane leaves were pressed flat into the sand of the Queen Square paths, like tile floors in long corridors.

Misremembrance

If I were painting I could
make a blur for the stairs
to rise from; it wouldn't matter
that I couldn't place them
anywhere on the ground floor
of the house, that they lift
in my mind of themselves
out of that vagueness, wide
and unbanistered, not closed in
by walls on either side, like
some stairway to heaven,
almost with clouds and angels
singing out of sight; I think
I carried my candle up them
though I was so small.

From halfway up such stairs
I could look down on that
scene where the front door
opens to let the flooded road
spill in across our flagstones
in a shining confined stream
that fits the back doorway,
the width of the garden path
then reaches the convenient
passing river and neatly
empties out; I have that
in my head where it makes
no sense at all, though
the road was flooded
and the river did pass by.

Swallow

Yes, it is probable
the earthquake will swallow you
if you sleep, when you sleep.

Slumber allows the necessary fissure.
You know how someone yawning
makes your mouth want to gape –
the ground catches that and
opens showing teeth.

You saw it in your grandmother's paper
(she reads you everything
as if you were a congregation
come to listen to the lesson –
here are the latest murders)

the Japanese city caught at
a slant between jaws of earth.

Your house will drop into such a mouth
like coins into a purse that's then
snapped shut. When sleep must come
you'll slip between those lips.

Though once you're almost utterly eaten
something turns over underneath –

Godney is made of water, its landscape
a lattice of bottomless rhynes, so a kick
of the feet can start you upward to
break into light and find it's morning...

Yes, it is probable
the earthquake will swallow you
if you sleep, when you sleep.

Borders

Down at ground level all the time –
on her knees, on hands and knees,
lying on her back under the belly of
the little horse she held up in one hand,
sent in a great leap over her and on
to gallop to the utmost of her reach.

The farm animals were all around.
Over there her sister crawled among
the cows on the old mauve carpet,
corralled by an inexhaustible fence.
From two windows white with sky
the light leaned wholly unobstructed.

A gate was wide enough for her hand
to enter, to stretch up to the elbow
and touch the several solid barns.
The laid-down doll was astonished
at the ceiling, a sheep knocked over
stared through its fellows to the wall.

Glose

I would never be lost
For all the world's beauty
But for a nothing in particular
That cropped up by chance.

                    ST JOHN OF THE CROSS

Begin with the furniture
making great rafts,
throwing up signposts
through the swirl of dusk.
The map in my head
put out an extra fold
to include a table
new to the kitchen...
So now I knew it all
I would never be lost.

But nothing in the garden
could be relied on
to retain its shape:
those trees in leaf
dropping their leaves,
growth, hailstones.
Mined by such anxiety
in the press of blossom,
I would trade indoors
for all the world's beauty.

A universe of detail
simmered there after all.
Once I was tall enough
to crawl on tops of things
those tines of forks
engaged me utterly
and how the clock hands
nudged themselves forward.
So I might have remained
but for a nothing in particular,

but for the hole I found
that shouldn't be there,
marring the completeness
of the thrown-down napkin;
void too deep and dark
underneath the clock,
the spider's web across it
gap thinly disguised...
then the gash in the gossamer
that cropped up by chance.

Aggression Diary

*They had become concerned about him and started
to keep an aggression diary.*

The leaning is a clue. Intent controls
the spine's tilt towards whatever.
See how he slants in his not-so-easy
chair, ignoring the burbling television.

Try to know exactly where he's looking.
The file shows the outside signs
of inner roaring can be small. A knuckle
gone white. The stretched-out throat.

*

Piranesi's *Carceri*: a man is racked,
the only sky above shows through a giant
treadmill, several pulleys dangle ropes
over indeterminate spiked objects.

Be careful what the eye feeds on
when it can't get out from inside
the walls and all the stairs lead
nowhere, the drawbridge drawn up.

And consider the weaponry to hand
in fire, bunched cloth, a stone dislodged...

*

Lightning ignited a dry tree in the garden.
He leaned still farther into the room
from his chair. Flames perhaps played
intermittently in the window glass.

The other spread his arms like a fierce
swan its wings, falling backward.
There was white rushing, flailing.
There were teeth on show on both sides.

And then, and then: what you would, expect
in cries and interventions, heat quenched
eventually, the furniture rearranged,
a return to the vertical through the house.

T.I.A.

Death begins when we are resting. Next time you are at a party,
serenely talking, take a look at everybody's shoes. You will see
them resting, horribly resting.

FEDERICO GARCÍA LORCA

He appeared to look long
into the shoe beside the chair
he might have fit his foot into
on another occasion. He appeared
to feel it was no such occasion
now. His gaze dwelt instead
in the well of the shoe – he would
know it again, it appeared,
know it inside out indeed.

I had asked him how he felt
and found his face stony. Something
had gone far back inside and left
a composed smoothed-over
effigy. Though this yawned twice,
yawned hugely, like a gulf.

The hand on his stick was
inconsequential – nothing to do
with standing up or sitting down,
but fact of nature as the creeper
long ago grown fat around the branch.

Then he settled into contemplation,
appeared to meditate upon
the nature of the shoe he looked into
beside the chair he sat in.
This felt like a long serenity.
And I, the others, so far outside it.

Till a face came up through stone
into his face, and his gaze beat
back against our gazes, the shoe
that had been a gulf forsaken.

NOTE: T.I.A.: Transient ischaemic attack, caused by temporary
interruption to the brain's blood supply.

The Right Side of the Cemetery

There were blackberries and I ate of them.
Is it the blackberries I need to enumerate?
Something there is to be clarified, listed and
ordered, to be ranged, arranged and counted,
but I don't know, I can't find, find out
what it is.
      There were blackberries, and I
trawled the right side of the cemetery for them,
taking from this bramble then that, stepping
past graves into the deep hedge that opened
to the sky in the best places, for the blackest
and sweetest ones.
      When did I slip from that
into enumeration, or the struggle to number?
I remember there were blackberries, and now
I find I am somewhere elsewhere, tallying
something or trying to get to where I'll know
what I must tally.
      There were blackberries,
then, maybe out of some recent dream that's
clogged and guarded from me, these things
which should make sense as soon as they are
properly remembered, the task that's set me
as in a nursery tale.
      I have slipped my usual
moorings and been cast adrift on this dream
by daylight, blackberries growing through
the plain assignment that somehow won't
get done, the job from the land of the dead
I can't look back and see falling away.

Going Back In

My art teacher suggests I go back in
and deepen the shadows with graphite.
That will make a more emphatic pit,
three-cornered at the drawing's edge.

'If you go back in with chalk pastel
the lip of that wave will appear to lift
towards the onlooker.' This proves to be
the case. I've returned to the page,

the once-white wilderness I'm colonising,
to catch a polar bear in the black pit
with three corners (and maybe bring ruin on
what so far is only a little blemished).

I can go back in and go back in, piling on
charcoal, soft pencil, conte crayon,
fixing one layer, reworking then refixing,
augmenting the sheet in strata like shale

(which is where they bore in search of oil).
The wave is slicked until it lifts no longer,
the polar bear goes down for the third time.
Perhaps all wildernesses should be left alone.

Maybe such whiteness should remain
unvisited, the tourist ship turned back
before the ice begins. Should I ever have
gone in to start with, ever begun to draw?

The Flower at Night

She was prim and folded.
like a flower at night
in the railway carriage.

She had pricked out a verse
at random in the Bible:
'Make a little chamber,
I pray thee,' it had read.

Illuminated grasses
standing beside the track
seemed to stream into
that coach's shadow as
forward streaks of light.

Though entropy driving
her bones could not be
gainsaid. Time turned the
cheeks of the Härkeberge
man astride Fortune's
Wheel from red to black.

Albertus Pictor's brushes
might have stroked such
lines of brilliance as the
grass's into his fresco's
church-lobby gloom.

'Make a little chamber
on the wall,' the verse said.
'Set for him there' stool,
bed, table, candlestick.

Several lit candles would
unfold the flower, retard
the darkening in her bones.

Cremated Girl

When they lay her out on black paper
we can see
what a pearly-queen she is

that can be put back in the jar as you might
spare buttons
saved for emergency repairs

All little plaques she's become who expected.
to turn to ash
sifted through someone's fingers

just as the juvenile gull anticipating whiteness
has to suffer
a mottled phase of grey and brown

and white whose patterns might have been
drawn around
paillettes of bone like hers

She remains a sketch anyway like the newer
Uffington horse
of minimal chalk lines

we must catch at sliding out of sight
upwards and over
the brow of the green distant hill

Slow Vocation

There's black for catching
and showing snowflakes –
velvet from a mourning
dress or a school slate
washed free of chalk.

The lady has laundered
her magnifying glass as well.
The day is a particular grey.
Probably it will snow and
she will fish for flakes

with a scoop of bombazine
or black lacquer box lid,
staying out in the cold
to pan for her specific
gold in the white flow.

Until one littleness looms
under the glass, stands proud
on the rods of velvet, and
she draws a sixth of it
at least, to multiply

once her fingers thaw.
Hers is a slow vocation.
For the snowflake on
its black platter neither
fritters nor dribbles away

but hurls itself from shape
to shape, rearranging six
angles ever more simply
till a plain hexagon
of ice becomes a drop

of water then water stain
on the bombazine, too fast
for her pencil to follow...
Begin again... To catch
the likeness of a snowflake.

NOTE: *Cloud Crystals*, with sketches by 'A Lady', which appeared
in the USA in the 1880s, seems to have been the earliest published
account of the intricate symmetry of ice.

Paper Washing

Somehow, she laid great sheets
of prepared paper down upon
the lit surface of the night water,
then took up after a time
the shadowy prints of its flowing
and braidings and hesitations,
hung them on white daylit walls.

*

The colours of this are silver
and graphite, dove grey, a steel
engraving. There's a fume
on the fields. The night is round
and enclosing and fragile as
some hunting Inuit's skin tent.

*

Isn't this the way
they throw down fine nets
on the water
then draw them back a little
like reins?
The way a tablecloth
is flung out in the air
then let subside
on its appointed surface?
The paper must hang
just a little underwater
if the river's ways of going
are to be printed there.
Let it slip from the bank
like a toy ship launched
then held to the end of its string.

*

Exposure
        is lightning over
the river
        the water revealed
all at once
        printed on paper
as an electric storm
            impresses
the retina
        with whole landscapes
there seemed to be
        no time to see.

Painting the Blind Man

A boy born blind, asked.
for his idea of beauty, named
fish moving through aquarium
water silent and separated.
He often stood by their tanks
not looking a long time, he said.

Reach your painter's fingers
into this dark water. The blind
man's hands are large pale fish
suspended just above his knees.
Your canvas is like a cistern
full of long-stored liquid.

'I don't know what they're doing,
fish. They give no clue. Though
some aquariums hum a little.'

It's hard precisely to distinguish
these painted eyes. Are they closed
or open? In such subfusc they
appear as faint thumbprints.

Once in a Blue Moon

Sleeping for peace among the blue hydrangeas

How deep. When you sleep for peace the avenues
shake out their hair of inordinate leaves
over the tents of protesters, over the sleepers' bags

Poppy and mandragora invade the processes
of – what? I have forgotten in this smoke
(and mirrors somewhere – don't they go
together, like demonstrators on the boulevards
lying hand in hand, flesh against its reflection?)

In the public gardens the previously mentioned blue
hydrangeas loom above their faces like moons.
Those elegant walks are corridors of makeshift
bedrooms. Day for night, and night for night

go on, an envelope around the sleepers,
the message posted: we are here and we dream,
again inordinately.
               (Note how this clots now,
almost stops.)
            A crowded dreaming rises
at right angles to the recumbent bodies
                          (but
that is why I falter, pause, tilt back from
the page. Someone said 'Never tell your dreams:
suppose the Freudians should come to power.'
Then remember the shapelessness you make
when you stumble awake towards words)

They mean to sleep a towering peace into the air
above the city. They mean it shall beat up against
the usual scene of down-falling judgement
with demons.
             The sheep and the goats lie side
by side and munch the blue hydrangea moons

Here Before

*They sigh for a PLOT. Oh, how they sigh. They are working
and slaving and fretting and stewing; they are sweating all over;
they are absolutely pining and dying for a plot!*
WILLIAM COBBETT, 1816

Four silk handkerchiefs
for the letters, a corn sack
to carry off books.
Manuscripts, pamphlets
in the King's Messenger's hands
at the cobbler's house.

Private secretary
to the Home Secretary's here
amid lasts, leather
shavings, baby drool.
That Committee of Secrecy
of the House waits.

*

'Disorderly house'
is the label for this room
where the reformer
speaks, we listen and
then speak what we think ourselves,
whatever it is.

*

Prove you are loyal:
take note of the complexion
of strangers, report
suspected persons.
The collection of flannel
waistcoats for the troops

(or greatcoats or boots)
will serve as additional
signal when those oaths
and signatures don't
show what is in your faithful
heart for all to know.

*

'Everything rung and
was connected. Everything –
not this thing or that
thing – was soaked in this
one event.' Look, listen
to its sodden toll.

*

Pub crawls are suspect.
In The Flying Horse he took
one drink. Two soldiers
spoke to him. The Ham
and Windmill in the Haymarket
hosted a meeting.

At The Bleeding Heart
his close associates were
Irish labourers.
Conviviality
in saloon and snug did
conspiracy's work.

*

He writes from Barnsley
to report 'The women all
talk mysteriously.
There's a general
expectation of they know
not what.' It's enough.

*

Since there was no trial
he calls his prison Bastille,
the print colourer
in a 'bog of straw'
without pen, ink and paper,
books or a candle.

Two years eleven
months with just a blanket in
the smothering dark
untried. His wife and
baby confined somewhere else
in the world outside.

*

The Home Office keeps
'disturbance books'. Whatever
they fancy goes in.
It's down to how you
read a thing. Equivocation
rules in England.

The Last Resort

On the beach of last resort
the impermanent wave. She was
beside herself there,

the pier like a pyre,
her boats burning behind
as the water went and went.

Sea slipped through her fingers.
The sand was the end of land
and her only landing strip,

the self beside her in tears
that could never extinguish
flame basketing her boats.

She resorted to slot machines,
tried a trip around the bay.
One self on the shore

saw the other, all at sea,
thread the legs of the pier
on fire, to dry her weeping.

Figure and Variation

1

I think of watching from hot-air balloon height
the figure come doggedly on
through the streets –
not looking up at the floating observer
who casts her unregarded shadow on the ground –
like that dog on the verge beside the creeping traffic
trotting on and trotting on,
passed and passed again,
with not even a sideways flick of the eyes
deflection from its forward onwardness.

Though in one dream he wore a stetson so enormous
it brought him up short
against still distant walls
as he turned almost on the spot
and turned the door (where I think I watched)
too narrow for an exit...

Still I thought he was at my door
as I turned into the street.

There was the time I saw him coming after –
not regarding me but coming the same way,
head down
with shopping bags –
and however I hastened or detoured
his even pace still brought him on.

2

Hot air streams upward, holding me in the sky.
I see the feral dogs like blood in the veins of the street.
I see them converge and part and his figure
going through, inexorably led like a dog to my door.

I feel the enormous impossible stetson above us,
a canopy. I feel how its crown fits him indirectly
as he moves always circled by the hat's exact shade.
It's a form of enclosure as well, shutting a door.

Perhaps his eyes are closed for he never sees me.
He's the kind of sleepwalker whose purpose,
though obscure, speaks its quality in his gait,
going on to somewhere (this turns out to be my door).

If I should chance to be ahead of him on that route,
I know he will never alter his steady going forward,
I know he must bear down upon me if I slow,
like Mr Hyde when he trampled the child. Close the door.

Anon in Three Postcards

He's passing – not necessarily on the way to somewhere.
He's out of focus, but it's clear
                                his feet are heavy
and he wears an overcoat and hat.
                                (I've come to see
a hat of some sort is mandatory.)

                                Kertész has used him
as punctuation,
                scale indicator for fence and tree
and inferred path across the New York square in snow.

        *

I enter Anon like a diver a tank:
                                no one knows
who took these other photographs

                                (but the same man
is here again
                and here again,
                                identity downplayed to –
at best –
                half profile half seen under a hat brim).

        *

Anon this anonymous becomes extraordinary:

without even a profile
                (hat seemingly resting
on his upper upraised arm),
                                he appears to plant a tree
in the very teeth of a hurricane:
                                he leans to it,

he presses the treetrunk down while its crown
whips above him.

> Their two slants steeple together.

> *

After the tempest he entered the bombed library
where anonymous had gathered,

> browsing the shelves.

(One has a finger hooked in the spine of a book
he might pull out,

> another has opened a volume.)

Behind their turned backs

> the brought-down roof
was piled as if for a great bonfire.

> The man we followed in
was passing through,

> a looker along the rows,
half profile half seen under the necessary hatbrim.

Man Entering Boiler House

(after Prunella Clough)

Here he is, waiting
at the doorway of the boiler house,
not stepping over the threshold,
but waiting to be let in,
for the dark to throw itself open
and invite.
      So far it's closed –
though the door's pulled back
inside – so far its blackness
is a surface no less smooth
or vertical than the plasterboard
beside it, asbestos white.

That there is anyone (me) behind
he is unaware. This is a private
transaction at the doorsill, there
will be a private translation
from foreground
          into the black.

Are you there, Mr Jones (boiler house
keeper)?
      Let me into the dark.
               Don't
let me in to the dark. It's better
here, not being let in yet.

If I cease to hold him steady,
back of his collar aligned with
the doorframe's upright, if
my gaze falters…
      I might find
he's slipped inside the blackness
he'd approached so circumspectly,
coming at it round the corner.

64

Has there ever been an entering
so strung out?
          This man without
an article at the generic boiler
house... action that binds them
slung between,
          rope bridge
suspended over nothing.

On the Way

When I came to our meeting
I walked up the hill towards it
and my walker's hill was taller
than the one for cars and buses
which sank below that pavement
as I rose towards the summit
till I might have stepped sideways
to the double-decker's upstairs
if it had stopped next to me.

I thought mine was the real hill
and that other they drove along
a pressed-on stamped-down
excavated contour – for the height
of the trees kept pace with me
as I climbed like a hang-glider
who hauled her struts and sails
to an apex she might take off from
trusting her weight just to air.

I'd remembered another route
the Ottoman bridge in Tirana
which formed the small hypotenuse
to a two-roads right angle and
short-cut its corner off – enough
of a function once the stream had gone
just to wind and three dry rocks
so the bridge was its own watershed
an up-ramp of river stones then down.

And I climbed and crossed it
and climbed it and crossed again
for the pleasure of breasting
the light as I crested its hill

and a sense that to be on the way
satisfied as suspension between
rough waters which had been and
floods to come – trusting that bridge
as arched substance in the air.

Fox Spirit

My path was crossed by the fox's path
in a reek part dog part game that was
just as defined in the air as an iron girder.

*

On the high back wall of the derelict lido
I saw the fox dance its way towards
the corner a cloud of pigeons burst up
from once that fox had dropped down.

*

Though only a little flyblown the dead
fox on the beach had a featureless head
like a white chalk drawing just begun
and its ears let the white light through.

The Plain Gap

I thought, if I was about to disintegrate
what would I fix my gaze on? And I saw
wind agitate one hair of the cat's eyebrow.
And I saw as she turned her head, how
her ear's shadow sharpened on the ground
among the rose's vaguer printings. I saw
that it was good. It was a good exercise.

So how would it be to be gone, a space
in the chair where I sat to watch wind
and sun? After the puff of smoke, that plain
gap where an object was – you are sure –
but is not anymore – and where is it?
The wind is in the cat's eyebrow, her ear's
faint shadow is darkening on the floor.

To Mr Jones (Boiler House Keeper)

Mr Jones (boiler house keeper), I am concerned.
that space presses on these edges,
                              glad
that space presses, extending the light
around all the margins,
                    but concerned because
it leans on the figures until their edges
blur, almost dissolve –
                    too much light
might consume this figure utterly.
                              There are
those here who've become only an elbow,
the half fan of a hand, back of the skull.

And even bones I thought were the deep inside
have their cavities, their deeper insides,
the channel for the marrow, or...
                              Mr Jones
(boiler house keeper), I saw in the museum
the split humerus of a pelican:
                              within
were three kinds of linen lace, in one place
like the chimney a spider builds...
                              as though
a spider could dwell in a pelican's wing,
set out its table, eat and have its being
deeply unseen there in the bone.

                              Mr Jones
(boiler house keeper), lend some darkness
to draw the lines, define these edges, keep hold
of the last shin bone set up against
this light rolling inward,
                         space rising inside.

That Bone

There was said to be an indestructible bone,
the cutting from which a whole body could be grown,
and would be, come resurrection:

Bone of Lutz the anatomists looked for –
not to be consumed by fire, not
to be ground between teeth of great beasts,

but like the germ in a grain of wheat,
like an elegant eternal white sperm,
a shining pin in the mould.

I wondered: was it component of my little finger?
Then the finger turned arthritic and I changed my mind.

Cheekbone, the smallest rib or, delicate in the ear,
stirrup bone, anvil – each had its own appeal
a moment... before derision came.

Oh I know it's not so – there is the new conviction:
we're stuff of galaxies and shall become
nebulae, comets, once we are stripped down –

not to the bone, but carbon's diamond glitter,
a speck of hydrogen dancing upon that pin
like an angel, helium iota floating away...

Still Life

Ah, but they moved before,
though you did not notice.
The bowl spun on one
invisible toe on the window
sill and the rose was
a sail or several sails
going going across the glass.

Come the Thaw

(Before the advent of polar exploration it was thought that speech would freeze in very cold climates. Versions of this conceit are found in Rabelais, Castiglione, Donne and Addison.)

We would never go into those icy places,
never swing towards the pole like
a compass needle. We know how
it is: there could be no living
there, words freezing as they
left our lips, freezing and
falling to the ground to
lie like crystallised
sweets till the
thaw came.

           When we might not be by to hear them.
We could not wait at our pile of words like
a cold campfire through midwinter, for we'd
freeze into pillars and trees not otherwise
to be seen in the icy places. Those
sweets would lie till there might
be a passer-by to take up one
or two and warm them in his
fingers. Then he'd hear
a word or two from
before the thaw.

           More probably the words would go
tumbling under the polar winds, jumbling into
nonsensical sentences. They'd spill across
the ground, spelling nothing said before
and melting out of order to tell
opposing stories. How could we
live like that: more than
half a year dumb, then
when the thaw comes –
knee-deep in noise
and no solution.

Dysphasias

1

To restore silence is the role of objects.
SAMUEL BECKETT

So. Without speech. I reach out to the object,
a round thing, round with thing. So thing. With.
So without speech I. Reach out to the object,
I cry inside. I cry. Inside. So without speech.
Without speech thing. Round. Round without
thing. Thing inside, I cry. Thing I. Round
and round and round I cry. Without. So I cry.
Speech thing. I reach thing. Out. With I.
I reach round thing to cry. Speech inside. I.

74

2

A picture held. us captive. And. we could not get outside it, for it lay in our language and language seemed to repeat it to us inexorably.

WITTGENSTEIN

'Moth,' she said,
and he turned his head to her,
smiling.

Velvet along the fractured
threads
      let us name
what had broken from the web.

Still hungry,
she repeated 'Moth'
more insistently.

They were at the window
and at the window
tapping
      till he turned out the light.

No child any longer
asked for a story
since 'Moth' was every word
under her flying finger.

3

I passed between the rows of perches on which parakeets from various countries were roosting... The parakeets stood out like his separate thoughts, each one materialised and attached to a pole.

CHARLES PELLETON

That between the perches
there were spaces
not occupied by his thoughts,
apertures in the procession
of parakeets on poles, places
where the mind lapsed.

That this freed the colours.
The green plumage
he called blue
with perfect confidence,
lazing under the apse
and looking out
on a nothingness
cooking like soup.

What if he let go
of memory's mooring poles:

prelapsarian
          Lapland
lapis lazuli
         lisped
Lapsang Suchong
             at her lap
lipsync-ing
       la-la-la.

The recollection unexercised
falls away by slow degrees
like a parakeet's flight
aborted through moult,
the aperture of air
crossed only by
lapsing feathers.

4

Reviewing language,
I am wrought up by how patient it is.
GEOFFREY HILL

By when were you hard done?

It was Monday, Tuesday, Wednesday, Thursday...
(I'm sweeping past the day again)

No, no. Why did the year?

(Motivation's a hard question)
Because, from here where we are at home
they went up to the moon. But don't believe it.

Where came the mountain from?
I was in the chemist's buying guns...
oh and a duplicator.

But how to the people who weren't there?

You try to copy the day on the ground.
(I can't speak at all
in the dark between street lamps)

Boiler House Watching

There are woods about the boiler house now, Mr Jones:

thin sappy treetrunks thick as grass
sieve every view
                    of its uncompromising rectangularity
                    (including that dark door).

So it's hard to believe in you
                    in there,
                              unseen,
                                        screened
by accumulating leaves.
                    There's no wisp of steam.

A watched boiler house never alters.

                              Then turn away
to white bladder campion tipping over,
the nest of wild strawberry
                    volatile as gas.

Do you look out at them, Mr Jones,
                              the boiler at your back?
If I turned round
                    suddenly
                    would I catch you in the act?

Does your gaze stop mutability in its tracks?

Let me tell you about the moss here –

                                  moist,
resilient.

        Let me sing what isn't boiler house,
to lure you out.

                (Which is maybe to note
                the path you tread this way
so as

        later

                to trace it

                        to the dark open door.)